Entrepreneurship

:: Author ::

Pareshkumar M. Thakor

PUBLISHED BY

The New Era International Publishing House
HQ. At & Po. Chaveli., Ta- Chansma,
Dist- Patan, North Gujarat, India, Asia.
www.iphouseindia.com

First Publication: 12th April, 2015

ISBN:- 978-15-12121-86-5

Price: Rs.750/- INDIA

$ 15 OUTSIDE INDIA

PUBLISHED BY

**The New Era International Publishing House
HQ. At & Po. Chaveli., Ta- Chansma,
Dist- Patan, North Gujarat, India, Asia.
www.iphouseindia.com**

What is Entrepreneurship and Who is an Entrepreneur ?

We often hear that so and so is an entrepreneur who has started his or her own business. It is also the case that when we hear the term entrepreneur, we tend to associate it with a person who has or is starting their own ventures or in other words, **striking it on their own**. This is indeed the case as the formal definition of Entrepreneurship is that **it is the process of starting a business or an organization for profit or for social needs**. We have used the phrase for profit or for social needs to delineate and separate the commercial entrepreneurship from social and charitable entrepreneurship. After defining entrepreneurship, it is now time to define who an entrepreneur is and what he or she does.

An entrepreneur is someone who develops a business model, acquires the necessary physical and human capital to start a new venture, and operationalizes it and is responsible for its success or failure. Note the emphasis of the phrase responsible for success or failure as the entrepreneur is distinct from the professional manager in the sense that the former either invests his or her own resources or raises capital from external sources and thus takes the blame for the failure as well as reaps the rewards in case of success whereas the latter or the professional manager does the job and the work assigned to him or her for a monetary consideration. In other words, the entrepreneur is the risk taker and an innovator in addition to being a creator of new enterprises whereas the professional manager is simply the executor.

Attributes of Entrepreneurs

Moving to the skills and capabilities that an entrepreneur needs to have, first and foremost, he or she has to be an innovator who has a game changing idea or a potentially new concept that can succeed in the crowded marketplace. Note that investors usually tend to invest in ideas and concepts which they feel would generate adequate returns for their capital and investments and hence, the entrepreneur needs to have a truly innovative idea for a new venture.

Leadership Qualities

Apart from this, the entrepreneur needs to have excellent organizational and people management skills as he or she has to build the organization or the venture from scratch and has to bond with his or her employees as well as vibe well with the other stakeholders to ensure success of the venture.

Further, the entrepreneur needs to be a leader who can inspire his or her employees as well as be a visionary and a person with a sense of mission as it is important that the entrepreneur motivates and drives the venture. This means that leadership, values, team building skills, and managerial abilities are the key skills and attributes that an entrepreneur needs to have.

Creative Destruction and Entrepreneurship

We often hear the term creative destruction being spoken about when talking about how some companies fade away whereas others succeed as well as maintain their leadership position in the marketplace. **Creative destruction refers to the replacement of inferior products and companies by more efficient, innovative, and creative ones wherein the capitalist market based ecosystem ensures that only the best and brightest survive whereas others are blown away by the gales of creative destruction.** In other words, entrepreneurs with game changing ideas and the skills and attributes that are needed to succeed ensure that their products, brands, and ventures take market share away from existing companies that are either not creating values or are simply inefficient and stuck in a time warp wherein they are unable to see the writing on the wall. Therefore, this process of destroying the old and the inefficient through newer and creative ideas is referred to as creative destruction which is often what the entrepreneur does when he or she launches a new venture.

An Entrepreneur is a Risk Taker

We have discussed what entrepreneurship is and the skills and attributes needed by entrepreneurs along with how they engage and indulge in creative destruction. This does not mean that all entrepreneurs are successful as the fact that they can become victims of creative destruction as well as due to lack of the other traits means that a majority of new ventures do not survive past the one year mark of their existence. Now, when ventures fail, the obvious question is who takes the blame for the failure and whose money is being lost. The answer is that the entrepreneur puts his or her own money or raises capital from angel investors and venture capitalists which means in case the venture goes belly up, the entrepreneur and the investors lose money. Note that as mentioned earlier, the employees and the professional managers lose their jobs and unless they are partners in the venture, their money is not at stake. Therefore, this means that the entrepreneur is the risk taker in the venture which means that the success or failure of the firm reflects on the entrepreneur.

Some Famous Entrepreneurs

Given this basic introduction to entrepreneurship, we can now turn to some famous examples of entrepreneurs who have succeeded despite heavy odds because they had game changing ideas and more importantly, they also had the necessary traits and skills that would make them legendary. For instance, both the founder of Microsoft, Bill Gates, and the late Steve Jobs, the founder of Apple, were college dropouts though their eventual success meant that they had not only truly innovative ideas, but they were also ready to strike it out for the longer term and hang on when the going got tough. Even the founder of Facebook, Mark Zuckerberg, as well as Google's Larry Paige and Sergey Brian can be considered as truly revolutionary entrepreneurs. What all these legends have in common is that they had the vision and the sense of mission that they were going to change the world and with hard work, perseverance, and a nurturing ecosystem, they were able to self actualizes themselves.

Entrepreneurship Needs a Nurturing Ecosystem

Finally, note the use of the term **nurturing ecosystem**. This means that just as entrepreneurs cannot succeed if they lack the necessary attributes, they cannot succeed even having them but living in an environment or a country that does not encourage risk or tolerate failure and more importantly, is unable to provide them with the monetary and human capital needed for success. This means that the United States remains the preeminent country for entrepreneurship as it has the ecosystem needed for these entrepreneurs to succeed whereas in many countries, it is often impossible or difficult to find funding, work through red tape, and ensure that the environmental factors do not inhibit entrepreneurship.

Principles of Entrepreneurship

Entrepreneurs need to follow some basic principles which would serve as guidelines and beacons for their success. Based on the research conducted over a period of three years and by interviewing more than 150 entrepreneurs, noted author and management expert, Bill Murphy came out with a book about entrepreneurship which was published by Harvard Business School. This discussion is based on the insights from this book and lists five principles that should serve as markers for both aspiring as well as existing entrepreneurs. One of the insights from this research is that most of these principles can be learned from experience and the process of starting a venture is an educational experience in itself. With this introduction, we can now move on to the five principles of entrepreneurship as put forward by Bill Murphy.

It is always not the case that Entrepreneurs should make money fast and this should not be the goal

It is important for entrepreneurs to test the waters before launching a new venture. This means that one must commit oneself to the ideal of entrepreneurship and try out new business models, and new forms and paradigms of transacting business. In other words, the entrepreneurs must not be in a hurry to make profits from the word go and instead, understand what entrepreneurship is all about. For instance, it is better to come up with a game changing idea instead of pursuing leads that are dead ends which means that entrepreneurs must be ready to be in the game for the long haul.

It is always better to find the right opportunity even if it takes time instead of chasing mirages

This principle translates into waiting for the right opportunity and at the same time, seizing the moment when the opportunity arises. Of course, we are not saying that entrepreneurs ought to wait forever for the right opportunity. Rather, the intention here is that entrepreneurs must ensure that they have the necessary foundation in place to capitalize on the opportunity and also must have an idea and a business model that would create opportunities in case they are finding it difficult to get the venture going. For instance, as the clichés about how opportunity knocks only once as well as if you do not find an opportunity, build a door so that you are ready when the opportunity arises can be taken to mean that entrepreneurs must both create opportunities as well as seize them when they arise. Another analogy would be that entrepreneurs must be ready with the fishing rods and the baits when they go fishing and if the river, sea, or lake is saturated, they must fish in waters that are "blue oceans" meaning that they must create new markets for themselves.

Invest in people and build successful teams

As with the previous principle, entrepreneurs must ensure that they have the right team in place before they start the venture. After all, unless there is a team in place, the venture would not be able to capitalize on the opportunities. Further, entrepreneurs must ensure that the team is passionate, committed, and most importantly, shares the vision and mission of the founders. In other words, unless there is a buy-in from the team with the founder's ideas, the venture would flounder. Apart from these, getting the right people who have focus, drive, loyalty, determination, courage, and consistency in addition to being motivated and creative are some requirements that the entrepreneurs can ill afford to ignore.

It is always not enough to have everything in place. Execution and Delivery are what matters

Have you ever got the feeling that a salesperson is engaging you in glib talk wherein he or she is trying to convince you to buy a product which is untested? Similarly, all talk and no execution would lead the new venture nowhere and hence, it is important for entrepreneurs to ensure that they walk the talk and deliver on their promises.

Indeed, it is not enough to have a game changing idea and a great team in place unless the entrepreneur knows the art of execution. As happened during the Dotcom boom, there were many startups with great ideas and equally great teams that promised the moon for anyone willing to listen. However, the fact that they failed in their businesses was mainly due to the gap between ideas and execution.

Therefore, the entrepreneur has to be a leader who walks the talk and understands the meaning of execution. Further, leadership means that entrepreneurs must not be afraid of failure and must instead, turn adversity into triumph and transform failure into a stepping stone for success.

Indeed, great entrepreneurs are those who are willing to trust their instincts and intuition and back themselves up when the venture is yet to fructify or even making losses. In other words, if you think that you have a great idea and are executing it well with the right team, you need to persist and keep going even when the conventional wisdom says that you are getting it wrong.

Entrepreneurs must be self actualizing visionaries

Ask any successful entrepreneur and they would say that while money is indeed important and profits are indeed essential, it is always not about the money or that making profits is the only thing that matters. Instead, great entrepreneurship is all about heeding the inner voice, creating jobs and opportunities for others, be conscious of societal prosperity due to the venture instead of having a me, myself only attitude, and most importantly, translate their vision into success.

For instance, there are many of us who have heard or come across individuals who gave up cushy jobs to find their passions and to follow and chase their dreams. Therefore, successful entrepreneurship is all about making a difference to the world and becoming a social messiah who would transform societies with his or her ventures. Finally, **entrepreneurship must be seen as a starting point to transform oneself and in the process become a change agent.** For this to happen, the entrepreneur must be both be able to fulfill environmental, social, and economic expectations from the larger system and at the same time, must drive themselves in the pursuit of their dreams. Indeed, the balance between inner aspirations and external expectations is the most important determinant for success.

Entrepreneurial Finance

Description

This discusses the various forms of financing for new ventures. It is indeed the case that any new venture would need capital and more often than not, entrepreneurs need significant capital for launching their ventures. Further, this is also discusses how Angel Investors have become important in recent years and examines how buyouts take place in the business world.

Need for Financing

Any new venture needs financing and hence, entrepreneurs have to decide where to get funding from, how to invest, and how much to borrow. This discussion is concerned with the sources of entrepreneurial finance which the entrepreneur has access to. Indeed, one of the central preoccupations for entrepreneurs is where and from to get the funding in order to kick start their ventures and hit the ground running.

Bootstrapping

This form of financing the ventures applies when entrepreneurs invest their own money, or offer stakes in their venture to individuals in return for their services, as well as includes other forms of financing such as delaying payments to partners, offering sweat equity to employees and other stakeholders etc. The important point to note about bootstrapping is that it can be actualized only when the entrepreneur does not need significant amounts of capital as all the methods mentioned above relate to investments that are limited in their capital mobilization. Another important aspect of this type of financing is that entrepreneurs typically offer equity in return for work done which is a non-monetized form of financing known as sweat equity.

External Financing

This type of financing is the most common for entrepreneurs and this category includes all the types of financing mentioned subsequently. When compared to bootstrapping where the entrepreneur raises money either from internal sources or by offering equity in return for work, external financing often involves sourcing capital from external sources which are tangible and immediately monetized forms of financing. Apart from the types of external financing described below, private equity or equity to large investors in return for financing is often the norm for entrepreneurs.

Angel Investors

We often hear the term Angel Investor spoken by entrepreneurs or mentioned in the business press. Angel Investors as the name implies are literally and metaphorically the Knights in Shining Armour to the entrepreneurs as they not only invest their own monies but are also known to guide the entrepreneurs in actualizing a successful business model. Indeed, Angel Investors are also known to invest in new ventures as a means of doing good for society as well as to share their wealth with new and up and coming entrepreneurs who they (The Angel Investors) think have a game changing idea. Moreover, Angel Investors in many cases are successful entrepreneurs themselves and hence, mentor the new entrepreneurs in the same way managers and role models mentor promising employees. It is also the case that in recent years, Angel Investors have invested nearly three times the amount of money as raised through venture capitalists.

Venture Capitalists

Venture capitalists differ from Angel Investors in the sense that while the latter invest their own money and often do so for giving back to society, the former invest in new ventures with capital that their professionally managed investment firms have accumulated from private investors. In other words, venture capitalists often act as representatives of individuals and trusts with capital to spare and do so for profit oriented purposes rather than the for fun investments by Angel Investors.

Further, venture capitalists need a compelling business model and its presentation by the entrepreneurs as they are in the business of investing for profit and hence, need to generate returns on their capital.

Buyouts

This type of financing happens when the entrepreneur sells his or her stake in the venture to individual or a group of investors. However, buyouts are also used to refer to instances when private equity firms pick up stakes in new ventures where the majority stake is still with the entrepreneur. Moreover, buyouts are latter stage investments which mean that by the time the buyouts happen, the venture is already into its growth phase or in the process of being on the road to profitability. Having said that, it must be noted that buyouts also happen when the investors realize that ventures have good assets which can fetch returns as well as have the potential to grow and generate value in the future. Buyouts can also be hostile meaning that the entrepreneur might be forced to give up his or her stake in cases where the private equity or the other investors decide that a change of ownership would be good for the venture. Finally, buyouts happen when the venture is also in the process of winding up as some investors might want to pick up assets on the cheap and sell them off piecemeal.

Entrepreneurial Ecosystem

What is an Entrepreneurial Ecosystem?

All of us are endowed with skills, abilities, and capabilities. However, the reason why some of us are so successful whereas others languish is mainly due to the way in which these traits are nurtured, encouraged, and enabled. For instance, we need to go to the right schools, have supportive families, and be mentored at all stages of our lives so that we do not make any missteps or commit blunders and mistakes that would prove detrimental to our progress. In other words, talent has to be nurtured if it has to flourish. In the same manner in which this happens in our individual lives, entrepreneurs too need enabling and empowering environments which not only ensure that their game changing ideas are translated into actionable pursuits but also ensure that these entrepreneurs have the necessary ecosystem in which they can thrive and prosper. In short, the entrepreneurial ecosystem comprises of the all the stakeholders including government, bureaucracy, funders, and consumers.

The Example of Bangalore

To start with, let us take the example of Bangalore, the Indian IT (Information Technology) hub, which is often referred to as the Silicon Valley of India. The reason why Bangalore became a hotspot for innovation and global corporations is that it offered a serene and salubrious environment (including the weather) in terms of readily available pool of talent, an unobtrusive government which unlike the Indian way of interfering in business did its best to keep out of the Indian IT industry and its growth, enabling laws and tax breaks that encouraged companies to reap the benefits, and most importantly, a thriving culture of innovation that was long the characteristic of the city before the IT industry made it its home. Indeed, all these factors ensured that Indian entrepreneurs such as the founders of now global brands like Infosys, Wipro, TCS, and other companies have an enabling and empowering entrepreneurial ecosystem which made them thrive and prosper.

The Original Silicon Valley

Of course, the blueprint for this ecosystem originated in the Silicon Valley of California in the United States wherein global behemoths such as Apple, Google, and Microsoft in addition to Facebook and thousands of other startups found that the entrepreneurial ecosystem there was eminently suitable for them to start their companies and prosper. Indeed, the fact that Silicon Valley is thriving despite the recession is an indicator of how the region has moved beyond the vicissitudes of the market and carved its own niche as a place where entrepreneurs can thrive. Further, China that has emerged in recent years as an entrepreneurs dream come true has followed the footsteps of Silicon Valley and has indeed, done better than it on many counts such as minimal governmental interference and maximum benefits which prove to be the right nourishment for businesses and entrepreneurs to thrive.

Components of an Entrepreneurial Ecosystem

Thus, for the actualization of an enabling and empowering entrepreneurial ecosystem, there need to be venture capitalists who would fund the startups and angel investors who persist with the ventures despite initial hiccups. Next, the government has to have laws and policies that would encourage entrepreneurs by giving them tax breaks, benefits, and land and facilities including roads, infrastructure such as international airports and the like so that global investors flock to these ecosystems. Further, the bureaucracy should not throw spanners in the works of the entrepreneurs through meaningless rules and regulations and instead, must speed up the decision making process as well as implement single window clearances. Moreover, there must be a talent pool of skilled and employable workers who would staff the startups and ensure that when they take off, the ventures have the necessary people to drive their businesses.

Why the Chinese are racing ahead?

Therefore, after considering the factors which go into making an enabling and empowering entrepreneurial ecosystem, it is clear that unless these aspects are taken care of, the inventors, and the entrepreneurs would take their business elsewhere. Indeed, if the example of China is anything to go by, it is that it has stolen a march over India on many of these aspects as not only does it offer the right ecosystem, it also ensures that the entrepreneurs are treated as heroes and heroic figures who are no less important than the politicians and other personalities who are regularly feted by society. In short, the lesson for any country is that global capital is country blind and region blind and just as the early bird catches the worm, the regions and the countries that are at the forefront of the race to attract global capital would win in the end.

Conclusion

Before concluding this discussion, it would be pertinent to note that some of the aspects which ensure an enabling entrepreneurial ecosystem such as land and water and infrastructure seem mundane in the light of the other aspects such as access to funding and laws and regulations. However, if recent events in India and other parts of Asia where the ecosystems for entrepreneurs are being built are any indication, these factors are as important to the entrepreneur as is the aspect that he or she needs to have a game changing idea and be ready to take it to the next level. indeed, the fact that many global corporations are now flocking to India after moving elsewhere for much of the last few years is mainly due to the change in priorities in the Indian policymakers who desperately need investments and jobs as otherwise, they would not only be left behind but also would risk the dropping out of the race altogether which in the globalized world economy is a surefire recipe for disaster.

Top Five Reasons why Entrepreneurs Fail

Introduction

Entrepreneurship is a tricky thing and unless, entrepreneurs are on top of the game all the time, the chances for failure are very high. Research has shown that not more than 10% of all new ventures go past the second year of their existence and that entrepreneurs often end up on the wrong side of success. This examines and discusses the top five reasons why entrepreneurs fail and these relate to funding, staffing, financials, operational reasons, and peaking too early or too late. All these reasons have the common theme of not managing the venture successfully and being lax or lazy as far as the nuts and bolts of managing the venture is concerned. Further, the other theme that runs through these reasons is missing the trees for the forest or not paying enough attention to details and at the same time, missing the forest for the trees or getting too bogged down in the details that the big picture is ignored.

Problems with Funding

The first of these reasons relates to the funding aspect. As we all know, new ventures and startups need funding at all stages of their lifecycle and hence, the entrepreneur has to ensure that the venture capitalists and the financial institutions back him or her from the word go and continue their assistance throughout the process. Often, it is the case that entrepreneurs fail to deceive as the idea which looks good initially fails to generate revenue or business leading to the venture capitalists developing cold feet and backing out from the venture. Apart from this, it is also the case that some startups and their founders do not anticipate the continuous cash flow that is needed to keep the venture afloat and we shall be discussing this in detail separately.

Staffing Issues

The second reason why entrepreneurs fail is related to staffing wherein the entrepreneurs often do not staff their ventures with the right resources and often fail to have the required resources when the venture takes off. For instance, in these days, it is the case that the ventures need enough resources when the projects roll in or when business picks up. On the other hand, having too many resources is also a drag on the venture as resources cost money and time to maintain. Further, not having the right resources because either they are too expensive or they do not want to take the chance of working for a startup. Indeed, gone are the heady days of the dotcom boom when just everyone and everybody wanted to work for a startup. Nowadays, many employees do not want to risk their futures by joining a startup whose future is uncertain.

Cash Crunch and Drying up of Liquidity

The third reason why new ventures fail is related to the financials or the managing of the cash flows which have been mentioned earlier. This aspect has to do with the fact that most entrepreneurs fail to anticipate the cash crunch which arises from the imbalance between accounts payable and the accounts receivables. Further, it is often the case that new ventures budget for revenues in the future now and this means that unless the revenues materialize, the venture would run out of cash. Moreover, it is also the case that the funding from the venture capitalists might dry up suddenly leading to liquidity problems. Indeed, though the venture might postpone receivables to the future, it cannot do the same with the payables wherein suppliers, staff, and vendors cannot be assured that the entrepreneur would honor the commitments as can be seen in the way the Aviation sector in India has seen some high profile closures in recent years.

Operational Mismanagement

The fourth reason why new ventures fail is the operational aspect wherein the entrepreneur fails to manage the nuts and bolts of running the business in an effective, efficient, and efficacious manner. For instance, many entrepreneurs often do not involve themselves in the ground realities of running the business and leave this to others wherein they concentrate on the bigger picture. Though we are not advocating that all entrepreneurs should micromanage their businesses, some amount of involvement with the day to day running is essential and indeed, critical. This means that the entrepreneur should handhold the business especially in the formative years or the first year at the minimum to ensure that there is no slip between the cup and the lip where the translation of ideas into the running of the business is concerned. Often, many entrepreneurs consider it beneath themselves to engage and involve in say things such as work schedules, human resources, and day to day financials and end up paying the price for such negligence.

Peaking too Early or Too Late

The fifth reason why many entrepreneurs fail is that their ventures often peak early or peak late leading to missing the curve when the right combination of ideation, incubation, and execution is actualized leading to success. For instance, some entrepreneurs have great and game changing ideas but peak too early meaning that they misread the signals from the market. This often leads to burnout and fatigue especially when the desired momentum has to be generated. On the other hand, some entrepreneurs peak too late meaning that they misjudge the timing when their products or the solutions have to be brought to the market. In both cases, the imperative is to ensure that the time from ideation to bringing to the market is just about right.

Though we have listed the top five reasons for failures of new ventures, there are other reasons as well including differences between the promoters as well as other personality clashes and issues.

The Role of Entrepreneurs in the Economies of Nations

Introduction

Entrepreneurs have a critical role to play in shaping the futures of the economies of nations. By creating value through starting businesses and ventures, they ensure that the wealth of the nations increases. Similarly, by exporting goods and services, they ensure that the economies earn valuable foreign exchange that is vital for the countries to import the necessary goods and services. In addition, by creating jobs, they ensure that the people in the nations are gainfully employed. Moreover, through their social causes and championing of public good endeavors, they actualize sustainability, social justice, and environmental responsibility. Perhaps the biggest contribution or the underlying theme that runs through all these contributions is their innate ability to innovate that ensures speedy and efficient development of nations and their economies. As we shall discuss in the next section, innovation is the differentiator between the success and failures of nations and their economies.

Innovation is the Key to Success

To understand the role and the importance of innovation, one must consider how Europe pulled ahead of China and India through the "great divergence" in the time of the First Industrial Revolution in the late eighteenth and nineteenth centuries. Before this, Asia was the dominant economic player in the world. However with the advent of the First Industrial Revolution, European economies took off in a big way. The reason for this was the entrepreneurial spirit and the innovative use of technology in the Continent which was responsible for its aggressive growth and subsequent dominance which continues to this day. Hence, this aspect which underscores the importance of innovation is the biggest contribution that entrepreneurs make in the development of nations. Indeed, the First Industrial Revolution is a testament to the individual hard work, collective innovation, and national renaissance which was all due to the astounding courage and initiative displayed by the entrepreneurs.

How Some Nations Prosper and others Fail

Turning to the aftermath of the world wars when countries had to be rebuilt and economies had to be developed, it is indeed the case that through the same qualities noted above, the entrepreneurs in some countries succeeded in ensuring that those countries emerged out of the rubble and the chaos to become successes. We are talking about Germany, Japan, and some Asian countries such as South Korea wherein the entrepreneurial spirit in addition to and with some help from the governments ensured that these economies pulled ahead of others such as China and India. Indeed, if not anything, the governments and the state should at least not come in the way of the entrepreneurs and stifle their creativity and innovation if they cannot enable and empower them. As we shall discuss in the next section, China realized this aspect sooner than India which again accounts for the differences in the development of these countries.

The Role of the State

As mentioned earlier, the unleashing of entrepreneurial spirit and dynamism in addition to innovation calls for an increased role of the state where it has to provide the infrastructure or the hardware for the entrepreneurs to succeed. Similar to a computer where the software sits on top of the hardware, the entrepreneurs can succeed by creating the necessary software only when the hardware is in place. It is indeed to the credit of the Chinese government and the leadership that though this realization came late, they were able to jumpstart the economy and ensures that their country becomes an economic superpower. As for India, the fact that it has realized that it is better late than never in ensuring that entrepreneurial energies are unleashed means that it is on its way to emerging from the abyss of underdevelopment and backwardness.

Entrepreneurs keep Economies going

Some experts in recent years have gone so far as to state that it is the entrepreneurs who keep the countries from collapsing due to social and political factors. Imagine how a typical day begins and plays it out in our everyday lives. No matter what would have happened the previous day, the first thing you get in the morning is the milk and the essential goods in addition to the newspapers and other items that are critical for everyday existence. Who delivers all these items rain or shine are the entrepreneurs millions of whom contribute and lubricate the levers of the everyday lives of peoples and shape the economic trajectories of nations. Indeed, the fact that it is entrepreneurs who keep the country from collapsing is made clearer when one considers how countries like India seem to bounce back from crises and step back from the abyss whenever there is a social or a political event that threatens the socioeconomic fabric of the nation.

Conclusion

As the founder of modern economics, Adam Smith, put it, it is the economic incentives of the entrepreneurs that ensures that you get bread on your tables every morning. In other words, the entrepreneur is not being altruistic when he goes about his or her business. Rather, it is his selfishness in making a profit that contributes to the economies of nations. Therefore, one must realize the fact that profit is not a bad word and that once everybody agrees that economic aspects keep us going, and then all of us would benefit since we would think rationally and objectively about the need to create an ecosystem for ourselves and by extension, contribute to the economic development of nations. In short, let us celebrate the astounding entrepreneurial spirit in ourselves and in others, and instead of creating impediments, let us ensure that we enable and empower ourselves and others in fostering creativity and innovation.

When Should Entrepreneurs Transition to Next Generation of Leaders

Why do Entrepreneurs Exit ?

Entrepreneurs launch new ventures some of which go on to become successful and game changing businesses. When the ventures become hits in their own right, some entrepreneurs hand over the reins to others whereas some sell their ventures or their stakes to other investors and businesspersons. Think of Sabeer Bhatia who launched Hotmail which was subsequently bought over by Microsoft. Hotmail was indeed a game changer wherein Bhatia brought to fruition the world's first free web based email service. This was a classic example of an entrepreneur who was impatient to launch other ideas and ventures though it needs to be mentioned that

Bhatia did not taste the heady success that he had with Hotmail.

Entrepreneurs who do not Exit

Of course, this example cannot be generalized to all entrepreneurs as many of them manage their ventures well into decades. For instance, Bill Gates of Microsoft is an example of an entrepreneur who managed it for decades before transitioning to the next generation of leaders. The reason for choosing these two examples is because they show how some entrepreneurs look for other ideas and to start new ventures whereas other entrepreneurs are content with managing the ventures that they helped incubate and bring to market. In other words, the question as to when should entrepreneurs exit their ventures if they do at all and the question as to when should they transition to new leaders and the next generation is something that depends on a combination of factors.

When is the Right Time to Exit ?

For instance, it was recently announced that the Indian IT (Information Technology) bellwether, Infosys, would no longer have any of the founders in executive positions and instead, the appointment of a non-founder as CEO (Chief Executive Officer) was supposed to mark the transition from the entrepreneurs to professionals from outside. Indeed, this decision was also accompanied by an announcement that the founders would no longer be called promoters and that henceforth; they would be treated as any other shareholders. The case of Infosys is an example of how the founders and promoters of successful ventures often face the dilemma of when to exit their ventures.

The need for Self Actualization

Indeed, except for family owned enterprises such as Fidelity, TATA group, and to a certain extent, the Reliance conglomerate, it is often the case that there comes a time in the evolution of businesses where the promoters and the founders feel that they have done their bit and hence, it is time to move on. In some cases such as Sabeer Bhatia, it is the thrill of launching new ventures again and again whereas in other cases, it is for the reason that many entrepreneurs would like to become angel investors and Sherpa's for the younger generation. This desire corresponds to the Self Actualization phase of the Maslow Needs Hierarchy model wherein the entrepreneurs feel that they have to become social champions and visionaries wherein their ideals can be used for the benefit of society rather than only for the firms that they have founded.

Entrepreneurs being forced out

Having said that, it must also be noted that some entrepreneurs are literally forced out of their positions because the investors and other board members feel the need for new faces in addition to corporate intrigues which are done by stealth. Think of the late legendary Steve Jobs who in his first stint at Apple was forced to leave though what happened subsequently was that he was brought back to turnaround the firm. Indeed, Jobs had the last laugh (literally and figuratively) as he engineered the transformation of Apple into the world's largest company by market capitalization.

Continuing the same point, there are other cases of entrepreneurs who have been edged out of their positions as promoters and founders. The reasons for this range from non-performance or simply the feeling that "he or she has lost their touch" and the aspect of the institutional investors insisting on professional management rather than family ownership. The lesson for us here is that it is better for entrepreneurs to quit or exit the firms when the going is good instead of clinging on to their positions and being forced out or realizing that they cannot add value anymore.

Divergence between Founders vision and Ground Realities

Another reason for such exits is that when the firms become too large or big, the vision of the founders and the ground realities in them become so divorced from each other that the founders realize that it is time for them to move on. This was the case with Infosys wherein it became a behemoth where ground realities were vastly different from what the founders wanted in recent years. Despite the best efforts of many stakeholders of Infosys, the realization that it was time to move on finally dawned on all concerned. This was driven by the fact that Infosys was widely perceived to have lost its Mojo because of this divergence.

Conclusion

Finally, some entrepreneurs plan the transition to the next generation well in advance and though this is an ideal that few can match, nonetheless, many experts believe that this is the best course of action for all concerned. Though examples of this kind of transition are rare, it has been known to happen in earlier decades wherein firms such as Unilever and Proctor and Gamble witnessed transitions from the founders to the next generation that was not a result of corporate battles but was instead driven by a conscious decision on part of the founders.

Venture Capitalists and Irrational Exuberance

The Dotcom Boom and Irrational Exuberance

For those who started their careers in the late 1990s and early 2000s would remember the Dotcom boom when the internet and software based businesses were expected to drive the future economic growth in the United States and elsewhere. Named because companies with a .com address were projecting high growth and endless revenues, this boom sparked frenzy in Venture Capital investing in these firms. However, the boom soon went bust leaving in its wake a string of failed companies, entrepreneurs who went bankrupt and venture capitalists who suffered huge losses sometimes of their own money. If there was a lesson from this boom and subsequent bust, it is that irrational exuberance in economies must be tempered with rational and cool headed thinking where people are not carried away by the transient and temporary.

History Repeats Itself

Having said that, the nature of the markets and economies is such that lessons are rarely learnt from history and within a gap of a few years, another boom in the US economy started where venture capitalists again started funding entrepreneurs with little or no experience in running companies. Before we proceed further, we would like to make it clear that we are not per se against investing in startups or funding brilliant ideas. Indeed, the nature of capitalism is such that disruptive innovation and creative destruction are the norm. However, what we are against is the mass mania kind of investing cycles where irrationality takes over and VCs start pouring in money in firms that do not have fundamentally strong business plans. Thus, what we caution against is irrational exuberance and illogical investing.

Are VCs Rational ?

One might very well ask, why do the VCs who are industry veterans with decades of experience in investing and funding startups go wrong? Further, why would they want to invest badly and lose even more badly? The answers to these questions lie in the mechanics of global capital wherein

"Easy money" and "high liquidity" means that the money has to go somewhere and this is where sometimes VCs tend to display irrational exuberance. Further, given the fact that returns on keeping money idle is less and the opportunity costs are more, it makes sense for these VCs to look to invest in companies that promise returns if only on paper. This is the reason why periodic bouts of market madness are witnessed wherein even the most venerated and experienced VCs tend to go wrong.

Hunt for Value Investments

Of course, this is not to say that VCs fund every entrepreneur who comes knocking. Indeed, research has shown that out of hundreds of applicants for funding, a handful are finally funded meaning that competition is intense. Therefore, it follows from this that VCs are always on the lookout for opportunities because they want to invest in companies with a bright future. Considering that they have to deal with "junk ideas" on a daily basis, they usually zero in on what their models of investing suggest would be profitable.

A Recent Example

A recent example is the Indian e-business portal Flipkart receiving a Billion Dollars in capital infusion from abroad. While there are many who question whether Flipkart would be able to justify such huge investments, there are others who believe that given the rather weak market for funding in recent years, this company has a solid business model and hence, can be trusted to deliver. The key take-away from this example is that we are of the view that such deals should be based on rational and logical valuations and not because the VCs have money to spare or because the future lies in the emerging markets. In conclusion, as long as there is money to invest there would be VCs and as long as there are VCs, there would be entrepreneurs on the lookout for funding. Therefore, the key point to note here is that it is important to find balance and not get carried away by the crowd.

Working for Startups - Pros and Cons

Why Graduates are Flocking to Startups

In recent years, many fresh graduates as well as experienced professionals want to work for startups as they feel that by doing so, they would be adding value to themselves as well as being part of an exciting and creative journey. The **first aspect about adding value for themselves comes from the fact that startups often work in an unstructured manner where out of box thinking and dealing with uncertainty are the norms**. This means that employees of startups would learn critical and essential problem solving skills which would help them later on in their career.

The **second aspect is because many feel that by being part of a concept or a venture that is new and represents a change from traditional companies would be challenging and stimulating to them**. These then are some of the reasons why many graduates want to work in startups which as recent placement season statistics show lapped up more than 50 percent of the graduating class in many business schools.

Some Risks of Working for Startups

Having said that, there are a few things to consider before committing oneself to a startup. To start with, there is no guarantee that the venture would succeed and be a source of stable income for the longer term. Indeed, the fact that many startups fail after a few years means that if you want to work for them, you must be prepared to take the rough along with the smooth. Next, many startups entice graduates with offers of stock options after they go public. The assumption here is that the startup if it becomes public would reap a windfall from the stocks. However, we reckon that this is a big risk because not all startups eventually go public and even if they do, they are not guaranteed of a booming rise in their share prices. Consider the example of Facebook which despite its high valuations flattered to deceive after its IPO or Initial Public Offering bombed in the market.

Do your Due Diligence

We are not trying to scare away the people away from the startups. Rather the intention here is to remind you that you must do your due diligence before committing yourself. Indeed, more often than not, startups offer exciting career prospects that include interacting with many famous people in the industry as startups are known to encourage even the newcomers to take more responsibility than they would get in established companies. Moreover, the thrill of seeing your work make waves is something that only an entrepreneurial venture can provide you. Apart from that, the fact that startups offer creative people a chance to put their creativity to good use. In addition, potential entrepreneurs who want to launch their own startups sometime in the future would learn a lot from working for such ventures in the initial phases of their career.

Conclusion: Does your personality fit that of the Startups ?

On balance, it would seem that the positive aspects of working for startups outweigh the risks. An important determinant of whether startups are made for you and vice versa would be your personality as well as your inherent tendencies towards risk and rewards. Working in startups is not for those who have many personal commitments because of the risks that were described earlier. On the other hand, startups are ideal for those who do not particularly like hierarchy and want independence. Therefore, check these aspects and determine whether you are a right fit for the startups.

Public Private Partnership Projects: The Indian Experience

Introduction

Infrastructure is crucial to the growth and sustenance of the Indian economy. With the country being a developing one which is just now beginning to enter the trajectory of economic growth that would catapult it into the league of developed countries, it is vital for massive investments to be made in infrastructure and the construction of airports, ports, highways, and public housing.

Since the Indian government is perennially strapped for cash, which is the case with other developing countries as well, there is a need for the private sector to pitch in and contribute to the development of the economy. Having said that, it must also be noted that for such private sector participation to actualize, they need to be incentivized economically and financially as well as assured returns on their investment.

Public Private Partnership (PPP) Projects

PPP projects are defined as partnerships between the state and the private sector, which cannot be called, either as complete privatization or complete governmental control. This means that the PPP projects are essentially partnerships that are formed for a specific purpose through the creation of a SPV (Special Purpose Vehicle) that has private sector equity as well as governmental stake in the form of land, water, and other resources that the government can offer the concessionaires to develop infrastructure around them and in them.

As has been mentioned in the introduction, PPP projects are the way forward for India, which has limited resources and hence, needs private sector participation as far as possible. Further, given the need to develop infrastructure on a war footing, the private sector with its deep expertise and experience in executing such projects would be in a better position than the government in this respect.

Problems with PPP Projects

Having said that, the experience of the PPP projects in the infrastructure sector in India has been a mixed bag with more failures than successes and the succeeding discussion highlights the problems and suggests some solutions. It would suffice to state here that future partnerships can learn from the successes and avoid the pitfalls that led to the failure of the other projects.

Perhaps the biggest problem that bedevils the infrastructure sector and the issue of the PPP projects is that the whole process is not transparent to the various stakeholders other than the governmental bureaucrats. Further, it is also the case that in instances where the PPP projects have failed, the blame game that ensues in the aftermath is usually directed towards the private players.

This creates perverse incentives for the other players who might reconsider their investments. Moreover, with so much of red tape and decision-making paralysis in recent years, investors are reluctant to invest in the PPP projects in India.

Apart from the problem mentioned above, the other risk that private players carry when they execute the PPP projects is that of the political uncertainty factor. It is indeed the case with many projects such as the Hyderabad Metro Rail, the

Airport in Bangalore etc that a change in the government meant a review of the project leading to uncertainty over its continuance. This can lead to losses for the private players, as they would have invested substantial amounts of money, which are at risk if the project is cancelled.

Given the pervasive nature of corruption in India, promoters and the private players tend to recoup the losses that they have incurred by way of bribes and lobbying to the public at large meaning that the costs are inflated without a scientific appraisal of such projects. Moreover, given the tentacles of the underground economy, which is estimated to be as big as the official economy, the sources of finance and funding are concerns for both the government and the other stakeholders. In other words, there is no mechanism in place that assesses whether the funding and the financing of the PPP projects is entirely from legitimate sources.

This is a tricky issue as PPP projects entail massive investments and with the chances of failure being high, they are high-risk projects. Therefore, there must be a proper mechanism in place where the risks are identified and allocated in a scientific manner. Shifting the risks on to the private players would be counterproductive as is the placing of too much risk on the government. As would be discussed later, a proper risk and reward system needs to be instituted for this purpose.

No PPP project can be executed without the sovereign guarantees extended by the government, whether at the state or at the central level. The experience of some private players in the PPP projects has been that governments change the terms and conditions o the contracts midway as well as withdraw them in some cases. Having said that, the governmental guarantees cannot become White Elephants as was the case with the Enron plant in Maharashtra.

Conclusion

The preceding discussion has made it clear that unless India embraces PPP projects wholeheartedly, it cannot make the "Great Leap Forward" which China did as far as infrastructure is concerned. Apart from this, the fact that the government is seen as the problem instead of the solution as far as the infrastructure sector is concerned means that the new government has its task cut out in attracting private players to invest in the infrastructure sector.

The preceding discussion has highlighted the problems associated with the PPP projects in India and has suggested some solutions. It is evident that most of the problems are systemic and structural in nature, which means that there is an urgent need to overhaul the archaic laws and remove the bureaucratic bottlenecks that stymie the PPP projects. Any discussion on the PPP projects in India is incomplete with a mention of the issue of corruption. Considering the fact that corruption at all levels adds costs to the PPP projects in addition to inflated project appraisals and other deleterious effects, it is indeed the case that this scourge must be tackled immediately.

Apart from these issues, the PPP projects must not be held hostage to political uncertainty and volatility. In other words, a conducive investment climate is the need of the hour in India. In conclusion, India is at the "take-off" stage as far as economic growth is concerned and if it is serious about joining the league of developed nations, it must immediately ramp up investments in the infrastructure sector and actualize the kind of growth rates that are being forecast.

Economics of Public Private Partnerships

Introduction

Public Private Partnerships or the PPP Projects are the answer to the development of countries like India that are starved of resources where the government finds itself unable to commit massive funds for infrastructure development and yet, needs such projects for economic growth. This is examines the economic aspects of the PPP projects by applying theory to the practice as is the case in India. Before launching into the discussion, it would be pertinent to note that PPP projects are here to stay and despite opposition from various quarters, it would be better if the decisions on such projects are made on economic concepts based inputs rather than on the whims and fancies of the players.

Incentives and Distortions

To start with, **private players must be incentivized to participate in the PPP projects**. Starting from the initial tendering to the contract singing and extending to the execution, implementation, and maintenance, at each stage, the private players must be assured of returns on their investment. For instance, it is common for many highways and other construction projects in India to be executed on a Build-Operate- Own/Transfer mode wherein the concessionaire is allowed to levy tolls and collect money from the motorists using such infrastructure. It is the case with the airports wherein the private players can operate them through revenues accrued by way of levies and user development fees.

However, in recent years, there has been a tendency by civil society egged on by vested political and other interests to agitate against the levying of tolls on highways. This creates a disincentive for the private sector as they can neither recoup their investment nor transfer the project considering the sunk costs. Therefore, the incentive system must be in place and equally important is the honoring of the contractual obligations by the government in a transparent manner.

Correct Estimation of Risk and Return

Apart from the incentives that must lure the private players, the **risk and return** equation must not be skewed against the latter and the reward system being offered to the private players must be appropriate to the risks that they are carrying. For instance, it is common in India to draft concessionaire agreements that are skewed in favor of the government in some cases and in favor of the private players in other cases. The determination of as to who is rewarded depends on a host of factors including the closeness of the private players to the powers that be and other forms of crony capitalism. This must be avoided at all costs and the risk and reward equation must be scientific in nature without allowing for biases etc.

The Problems of Moral Hazard

Having said that, it must also be noted that in some cases, the Indian government has been bending over backwards to some private players especially in the case of ports and airports. This has taken the form of arranging for soft loans and deferring the payment period as well as bailing them out when necessary. This creates a problem of **moral hazard** wherein such concessions to some can be demanded by the others as well. The world witnessed the mega bailouts of the big banks in the aftermath of the 2008 financial crisis. Some economists decried such bailouts as being morally hazardous as they reward bad behavior and penalize those who have played by the rules, it is indeed the case that the Indian government would well be advised to draw lessons from this and ensure that it does not fall into this trap.

Mapping Demand and Supply

Next, and perhaps the most important aspect as far as economic theory is concerned is that there must be a balanced demand and supply equation as far as the PPP projects are concerned. Recent research indicates that the construction industry has been overly invested in leading to excess supply in the absence of adequate demand. For instance, the inventory buildup in some of the infrastructure projects such as public housing and the creation of SEZs or Special Economic Zones reveals that massive investments have been made in these sectors that have resulted in oversupply.

Allocation of Resources

Fourth, the **guns vs. butter** dilemma is something that the Indian government grapples with as far as PPP projects are concerned. Considering the fact that India is still a developing country and hence, needs to invest massively in creation of social infrastructure, it is faced with a dilemma of channeling investments and partnering with the private sector according to the priorities that are determined by the above aspects. However, it is also the case that India needs modern infrastructure such as world-class airports and hence, cannot shy away from inviting private participation in such ventures. At the same time, there have been vociferous protests against excessive investments in infrastructure that ignore the needs of the average person. Therefore, it is indeed a balancing act for the government as it tries to grapple with this dilemma.

Conclusion

As can be seen from the above discussion, PPP projects have to be evaluated financed, and revenue generation done based solely on the economic aspects by applying theory and not because of political or other considerations. For long, the PPP projects in many developing countries have been hostage to political compulsions and hidden agendas of vested interests. It is high time all the stakeholders agreed on evaluating and executing the PPP projects on the basis of the points mentioned in this discussion rather than on the basis of vote bank politics and crony capitalistic considerations.

Youth Entrepreneurship - An Overview

Youth is the Future of every nation & inheritors of the earth tomorrow. This statement stands true in every sense. When a country has a healthy youth population, you will find the country making headway in terms of overall development and progress. A country with high aging population and lower youth population has a lot of problems to content with that can slow its growth.

The world today has transited into a 'Technology Era'. Technology has enabled progress in all fields and all societies. Technological revolution has changed the face of lives of people bringing healthcare, information and connectivity to even the most remote areas that were hereto isolated.

Globalisation has brought countries together and created entire world market. We are seeing a lot of changes in the international political map of the world. Countries are beginning to show determination to move from the old age monarchies and dictatorial regimes towards democracy.

Progress and challenges go hand in hand. One of the major challenges faced by most of the countries in the world today is to do with Youth unemployment. The overall unemployment rate is growing at an alarming speed. Amongst the unemployed, the unemployment of youth seems to be alarming. The current global youth population is estimated to be at 1.5 billion of which 620 million are employable and ninety percent of this population live in developing countries. Countries like India and China have a fast increasing youth population and the rate of unemployment too is rising rapidly. As per ILO's prediction approximately 660 million youth will be seeking employment by 2015. The youth unemployment is higher measuring up to 50-60% in Asia.

The above figures stand to reveal the fact that Global youth unemployment could boomerang to become a global crises causing social and economical impact on all countries besides pushing the economies and progress backward. Though every government as well as World Organisations do frame policies and promote schemes as well as funds to promote youth employment programs, the quantum of such effort is negligible when compared to the huge numbers.

Governments are focussed on looking at framework and strategies to creating new jobs and increasing employment rates. However there is an urgent need for the policy makers to look specifically at the Youth unemployment and related issues. **In some of the countries youth entrepreneurship is being recognised as a**

promising alternative and is being actively promoted by various agencies. If promoted actively, Youth entrepreneurship can help sustain growing economies; integrate youth into the workforce besides leading to overall development of society.

Entrepreneurship in any society is a sign of progress. The IT business in US has been the bedrock for youth entrepreneurship and created stars and multi-millionaires in Bill Gates, Steve Jobs to Google's Sergy Brin and Larry Page and many more. There are similar such stories in other countries too. However, the need of the day is to create many more stars and make available the opportunities for every youth to dream big and try their hands at entrepreneurship.

Youth entrepreneurship has an impact on social as well as cultural and economic progress of the society. Building an environment that promotes creatively and provides opportunities for entrepreneurship calls for multi pronged strategies implementation and involvement at all levels including Government, industry, political, social as well as educational sectors.

Working towards Youth Entrepreneurship programs can help solve as well as avoid a lot of problems that are currently staring at the countries and pave way for a better future and progressive societies world over.

Youth Unemployment and Causes

Youth unemployment is being recognised as one of the problems that could grow into global proportions in the coming years causing social and economical problems for the societies. Youth entrepreneurship is being look at as an alternative besides other methods of creating employment opportunities. However, there is a need for global recognition and promotion of Youth entrepreneurship on sustained long term basis for this field certainly holds a promising future.

Revolution in technology and the resultant growth in all fields and globalisation has impacted the World. Developing countries like India and China are growing rapidly both in terms of economic development as well as population. Growing economies provide ample opportunities for services and provide opportunities for entrepreneurs to set up small enterprises in different fields. There are huge opportunities for individual enterprise in IT Services, Financial services, Travel and Tourism, Food, Supply chain, Health care services and many more fields. While some country's economies are not growing and the unemployment is growing, in the developing countries which are registering higher economic growth, there is no impetus for growth of youth entrepreneurship.

Reasons and Causes of Youth Unemployment & Entrepreneurship

1. **Socio-Cultural Factors as Inhibitors to Entrepreneurship**

In some of the countries the social and cultural outlook of the societies may not encourage initiatives and entrepreneurship. Many societies expect the youth to obtain education that enables them to get a job and earn salary to support the family. Economic compulsions too can push the families to encourage youth to look for jobs and not look at opportunities. In some cases certain caste or class of people are habituated to practicing certain occupations and thus entrepreneurship becomes a prerogative of certain sections of the society. Some other societies are risk averse and tend to play safe, while many communities believe in their children pursuing defence services opportunities or social service opportunities and so on.

In societies where the incidence youth rebellion, revolt and violence is very high due to economic situation as well as due to the cultural outlook, youth may be wasting their time neither pursuing education that helps them gain employment nor trying their hands at hands at entrepreneurship in the face of too many obstacles and hurdles in the society.

2. **Economic & Political Factors**

Economies which are not growing are grappling with huge unemployment problems and this is affecting the youth too. When the economy is down and the business is not doing well, there will be no opportunities for small entrepreneurs to provide services to support the economy and business.

Political will and focus to focus on youth in the country and to create a positive environment that encourages youth to dream and work towards realising their dream is very much necessary in any society. It is the political will that can spearhead the Youth revolution. Absence of stability in the political situation of the country and the political party's outlook towards this area can make or break the youth entrepreneurship's growth.

3. Policy framework

Government policy and framework in the country helps identify and build the base for youth entrepreneurship. The policies need to encourage and provide opportunities as well as assistance and environment to give impetus to youth entrepreneurship and have got to be implemented at national, regional and local levels. Policy directives will need to engage the business, banking, educational and other sectors to be able to deliver definitive steps to encouraging and aiding youth entrepreneurship. Lack of such policy framework can hinder the growth and initiative in the youth.

4. Industry Support & Patronage

In any industry, it is largely the business sector that provides opportunities for support services and creating new networks of business enterprises. Similar to their role in social responsibility, Industry can create a very strong platform to help develop the youth and give them the support and guidance as well as opportunities to the youth. In society where the industry enterprise is not very significant or not very active, there can be no encouragement for youth entrepreneurship.

5. Education System & Orientation

In most of the countries today the education system is geared to enabling the youth to pass out with their qualifications based on academic knowledge and prepare for seeking a job. There is little or no focus on building and equipping the students with leadership, building awareness and giving them training for entrepreneurship. Of late there is a trend to introduce specialised courses and training modules on entrepreneurship in many of the universities. In most cases the students do not attempt to think out of the box as they are not equipped with the necessary skills.

6. Finance & Business Support

One other biggest hurdle faced by each and every entrepreneur is the lack of financial backup and funding as well as guidance required to incubate new business. Most often those who attempt to start any enterprise do so borrowing from family and friends and dipping into their saving. After a while the business starts to suffer due to lack of funds and they end up in a debt trap.

Banking and financial assistance should be made available easily and this can happen only with the active support and engagement by the Government. Nowadays venture capitalists are funding new enterprises. However this is available to very few and not to the larger sections of the society.

Cultural Dimension to Youth Entrepreneurship

When we refer to a country's resources and wealth, we refer to their economic position, the availability of natural resources, financial status as well as the state of technological growth etc. However not much attention is given to assess the human capital especially the youth capital. It is true that youth is the future of every nation, a fact that most people tend to forget. Every nation seems to be caught up in chasing current priorities and not giving sufficient attention to the development of youth which is going to be the future human capital.

If the youth have to be developed as a resourceful and innovative future generation, the effort has to be put in by all including family, society, community, schools, colleges as well as industry and government too. As such each of these have a significant role to play in contributing to creation of Youth Entrepreneurship.

Family and Community play a very significant and important role in directing and guiding the youth in pursuing their future. Normally communities and societies that have had to struggle or have been striving for economic sustenance are seen to promote a view that the youth should take up a job and start contributing to the family's income and help with the expenses.

Most of the third world countries and the rural youth population face this reality. The social and cultural background of the families and community either support or inhibit enterprising culture and behaviour. A community that is sensitive to the development of aspirations of the youth nurtures the same and creates a trend for self-employment. We see from the recent history that American society has promoted a culture of youth entrepreneurship resulting in hundreds of YE in the Silicon Valley as well as other areas. Europeans especially the Youth in UK seem to be motivated towards taking up jobs and not necessarily striving to be on their own. A culture that is forgiving and allowing one to make mistakes and learn from them breeds Youth Entrepreneurship and creativity. The cultural outlook of societies at large is a result of history and years of tradition that have been passed on from generation to generation.

At micro level, the outlook of the community and family towards money, standard of living, education as well as their aspirations guide their thought process for the Youth too. A prosperous and progressive society creates a healthy environment and demand for products and services thus creating business opportunities. The awareness of importance of education and their traditional view to education too plays an important part that helps the youth dream, aspire and strive to explore new ventures and opportunities to grow their knowledge, allows free thinking, exhibit their talent, strive for economic independence as well as work for social services or inhibits them, their thinking and growth.

Historically China, India and Persia as well as Europe were the centres that promoted Education and advancement in all fields of science and technology. Modern times have seen America and Europe becoming the international educational hubs drawing thousands of students from all over the world. The outlook of the American and European Universities have shaped the outlook of its students who have turned out to be progressive, enterprising and excellent human beings who have contributed to and given back to the society at large. This cultural outlook and the resultant affect on the youth have prompted parents of all nationalities to send their children abroad for higher studies. If scientists and doctors as well as IT professionals are always looking to migrate to America from the rest of the world, it is because of the freedom and opportunity as well as the spirit of Entrepreneurship that the country provides for the youth.

Each and every community as well as society tends to have its own cultural outlook that is aggressive, peace loving, progressive, liberal, conservative etc. The outlook of the community has a bearing on the overall lifestyle and thinking of the younger generation as well as the outlook and progress of the nations too.

Coming out of the cultural mindsets, nations today have recognised the need to build and train their youth by providing education and skills necessary to make them job creators rather than job seekers. Several programs and funds have been provided by the Countries Governments as well as the World Organisations like ILO, UNESCO and others. However the effort towards building awareness and providing training is miniscule compared to the need at the global levels. While the Governmental agencies are trying their best to promote Youth Entrepreneurship, there is a lot more that NGOs and Industries as well as Educational Institutions can do both at national and international levels. Collaboration and Collective participation can help make a better future for the coming young generations.

Different Types of Youth Entrepreneurship

Year 2001 goes into the annals of history as the most significant year of contribution made to YE through creation of Youth Employment Network, an initiative and partnership between United Nations, ILO and the World Bank. YEN was the outcome of the millennium summit that resolved to create and provide decent work opportunities for the Youth across the globe. YEN provides the global platform to exchange ideas, plans and framework to improve work opportunities for the youth through a network of developmental agencies, governments, business and economic communities as well as Youth groups and NGOs.

YEN has identified Employability, Equal opportunities for young men and women, Entrepreneurship and Employment creation as the four goal posts for furthering Youth employment.

Understanding the subject of Youth Entrepreneurship begins with trying to identify and define the different types of Youth Entrepreneurships. While some of the academicians have categorised Youth Entrepreneurship into Economic, Social, Public Entrepreneurship and Intrapreneurship the list of categories is exhaustive. With recent studies and based on the differentiation in the behaviour and attitudes, roles, functions, industry and many more relevant characterisations, new categorisation of Youth Entrepreneurship has been put forth by the researchers. We shall enumerate some of the important categories as defined by the new generation scholar Clarence Danhof.

1. Innovative Entrepreneurship

The so called mavericks that are able to think out of the box, innovative new methods, processes and create new business opportunities out of their innovative ideas are known as Innovative Entrepreneurs. Currently we can name dozens of Innovative Entrepreneurs in the world. If Bill Gates and Steve Jobs made history in the recent past, they are being fast replaced by youth entrepreneurs like Jack Dorsey - founder of twitter, Sergey Brin, Larry Page of Google, Mark Elliot Zuckerberg who founded Face book.

2. Imitative Entrepreneurship

Most of the entrepreneurs in the developing countries and under developed countries who bring home tried and tested technologies from the developed world and establish them in the home country come under this category.

3. Fabian Entrepreneurship

Youth entrepreneurs who take on the business from their previous generation and manage to grow the business without taking any major risk of deviating into new areas but improving efficiencies, processes and scale of operations etc are called Fabian Entrepreneurs.

4. Drone Entrepreneurs

Drone Entrepreneurs are the first generation Entrepreneurs who manage the business handed down to them and continue to look at running the enterprise smoothly without taking any risks. This kind of attitude may be said to be an individual train of the Entrepreneur that leads him to manage the inherited business in a steady mode.

Further Classifications of Youth Entrepreneurship

Entrepreneurship is an outcome of a lot of factors including values, beliefs, attitudes, innate spirit, inborn leadership, and influence of environment, family, skills and many more. Therefore categorization of Youth Entrepreneurs can also be classified into several types based on various factors. Some of the classifications have been arrived at based on the type of business, based on technology, based on geography [Rural & Urban], as per Gender, scale of operations etc. Business entrepreneurship which is one of the significant and dominant categories can be further sub divided into Business, Trading, Industrial, Corporate, Agriculture, Retail, Service and Social Entrepreneurs.

Role of Society and Culture in Shaping Youth Entrepreneurship

Building Your Entrepreneurship everywhere is the necessity of all nations. There is recognition of the fact that the soft power of the future is in the country's youth and moulding them is important to ensure overall progress of the society. Youth unemployment and absence of Your Entrepreneurship developmental programs creates not only economic problems in the society but leads to several social problems too.

Understanding the background and the Your Entrepreneurship culture in any society is a very complex subject. Lot of research has gone into studying the influence of cultural attitudes of a community, a society or an ethnic group and the national political as well as economic environment and their mutual interactions affecting the attitude of the youth towards Youth Entrepreneurship.

The study of growth potential of Your Entrepreneurship with reference to the environment in the society alone does not give a complete picture. It is important to understand in detail about the issues, approaches, barriers and factors affecting or inhibiting Youth Entrepreneurship in the country, for any initiative to develop Your Entrepreneurship would start by removing the barriers to growth of Your Entrepreneurship.

One of the significant studies on Youth Entrepreneurship and the influence of culture at the workplace and development of values among the Youth has been put forth by Hofstede. He has proposed a four point model that influences the Youth Entrepreneurship in the local work environment. As per him the cultural elements of 'Uncertainty Avoidance', 'Individualism', 'Masculinity' and 'Power Distance' influence the attitude and thinking of the Youth with reference to their personal goals and careers. It is seen that the youth's behaviour and thinking pattern is shaped by these four factors. An individual's attitude and approach towards achievement and pursuit of his goals and what he wants to be in life, risk taking ability and approach, as well as the acceptance of personal, family and social duties are shaped in accordance with his understanding and reactions to these four factors. In societies which are accepting uncertainties, the youth are more likely to be more risk taking and trying their hands at entrepreneurship and aim for higher achievement. History shows that American society is more open to risk taking and accepting un certainties as compared to Europeans who are averse to taking risks and facing uncertainties. They would prefer to have a stable and steady job than try their hand at new ventures. It is said that

Americans are afraid of failure and the culture is such that they are not likely to accept failure at any cost and will do anything to make their ventures a success. A good example of power distance or hierarchies is evident amongst the Japanese, for it is embedded in all aspects of their culture. In communistic countries the approach to entrepreneurship is a lot different compared to other cultures. The societies have grown with the belief in the State providing for their welfare and such attitude can inhibit a aggressive entrepreneurial drive.

The individual's perception of what his family and friends think or opine about entrepreneurship has a crucial role to play in his views. Besides, the view of the family, their support and the society with regard to failure is also a very important factor playing upon the young minds and framing their opinion. Family's support is very essential because in most cases the Youth would need to borrow initial finances from the family and friends. The family's attitude towards education and other careers in fields like medicine, engineering etc are also likely to dominate the Youth's mindset towards entrepreneurship. It is quite likely that the families will be ready to take loan and fund the youth's professional education rather than funding for a new business venture where risk is involved.

Surprising but true is the fact that the society's views about business entrepreneurs as prospective bridge groom can also become a deciding factor promoting or inhibiting Your Entrepreneurship. In some societies people prefer to marry their daughters to persons holding Government jobs thinking that the jobs are secured and permanent as compared to a self employed individual. Normally professionals like lawyers, doctors and scientists are seen to be the most preferred as bridegrooms. Parents of eligible girls are likely to associate self employed youth with certain values like corruption, straight forwardness, honesty etc. These are but purely individualistic opinions but they are still relevant in terms of shaping the Your Entrepreneurship in the society.

Building Youth Entrepreneurial Culture

Recognising the need to invest into creating and building Youth Entrepreneurship in the country, Governments and international agencies have embraced long term agendas to co-operate and collaborate in formulation of strategies and implementation plans for building training programs, building awareness amongst the youth and the families and empowering the youth with the required skills and knowledge to pursue entrepreneurship as an career option.

Building Youth Entrepreneurship through Education

Creating and building a Youth Entrepreneurial culture in the society calls for two pronged strategy. The first and foremost platform for building the awareness and initiating the Youth into the concept of Youth Entrepreneurship is by investing into Entrepreneurship Education. This involves creating and including Entrepreneurial and Management studies at all levels of education. The action plan in this section includes building the content and syllabus and making it available to the teaching communities, training the teachers and counsellors to become Entrepreneurial educators and providing them with the infrastructure and facilities required.

One of the most significant aspects of Enterprise education is to involve industry and business organisations into the Youth Entrepreneurship programs at College level so as to provide an opportunity for the Youth to get hands on experience and increase their awareness of the business and economic environment.

Promoting Youth Entrepreneurship Culture using Media & PR

Apart from introducing Enterprise education, the Youth Entrepreneurship strategy has got to address the issue of building Entrepreneurship awareness and culture amongst the youth. **Creating an Entrepreneurial spirit amongst the youth can be done with the help of media and communication**. Holding awareness programs, Orientation camps, group discussions, specific campaigns, promoting Youth Entrepreneurship events at all possible platforms as well as instituting young achievers awards and competitions are some of the effective ways of building the Youth Entrepreneurship Culture. Youth meets, Seminars, Conferences, Festivals, fairs as well as using print media in the form of brochures, banners, coverage in magazines and interviewing successful entrepreneurs and young starters in the media and many more such PR exercises are sure to build the awareness and enthusiasm amongst the youth as well as change the perception of Entrepreneurship in the family, society as well as at the individual level. There are also available several business case based simulation games and competitions that invite Youth to participate in creating Business plans etc. These are of course relevant to nurturing the Youth entrepreneurs who are already interested and set on starting their own enterprise and are pursuing business management education to equip themselves.

Successful Entrepreneur Role Models - The Best Youth Entrepreneurship Ambassadors

Theory has it that a significant part of learning in an individual happens through role models. It is a fact that every youth or individual grows up having one or more role models who they try to emulate in all respects. Quite a few values, thinking patterns, attitudes etc are imbibed by the individuals based on their role model's personality and character. Therefore engaging successful youth and adult entrepreneurs as Youth Entrepreneurship ambassadors would be one of the best strategies to motivate and build Youth Entrepreneurship culture amongst the youth. When a Young Entrepreneur receives a reward, his success story gets to be known to everyone. Seeing someone taking up entrepreneurship and going on to become a successful entrepreneur does make other aspirants more confident of trying his or her hand at starting on their own. Success always prompts people to take risks and help the families and society accept the idea of encouraging the youth to take up entrepreneurial ventures.

Engaging the industry and the successful business entrepreneurs in addressing the youth, promoting Youth Entrepreneurship, interacting with Youth at schools, colleges as well as all other platforms can affectively and collectively build an environment that is conducive to growth and development through Youth Entrepreneurship.

Building Youth Entrepreneurship Through Education

Though people say and believe that Leadership is born and cannot be learnt, the saying may not hold ground in all circumstances. When it comes to Youth and Entrepreneurship, a sustained effort to build leadership or entrepreneurial ship definitely helps and yields results. Youth Entrepreneurship is an amalgamation of attitude, character, behaviour, passion, natural orientation towards entrepreneurship and leadership sharpened by training and building awareness and skills necessary to become entrepreneurs. A good leader alone may not make a good entrepreneur and a good entrepreneur need not necessarily be a savvy leader. It takes a lot more to become a Youth Entrepreneur.

Entrepreneurship as an attitude can be nurtured and developed in the youth at early formative stages. Integrating Entrepreneurship development as a part of the high school curriculum and expanding the same stream into college and university levels helps to give impetus to the budding entrepreneurial minds and allow them to give shape to their ideas and dreams. **Sustained educational and awareness building programs combined with training in business skills helps develop a culture that promote enterprise**.

Canadian Government's effort at building Youth Entrepreneurial ship and the 'Youth Entrepreneurship challenge, Quebec's - A three Year Action Plan' is a benchmark in the area of building Youth Entrepreneurship through education. Starting in 2003, the Government has invested over 20$million to building Entrepreneurial culture amongst the youth. As per the plan the committee works extensively with the education sector including Primary, Secondary as well as University levels and other student and teacher communities to integrate a holistic approach towards introducing Entrepreneurial education as a part of the curriculum. They have also conducted extensive training sessions covering educators and counsellors to include entrepreneurship development agenda in their teaching and syllabus. As a part of the initiative, various initiatives including conducting awareness campaigns and trainings at family and community levels, introducing entrepreneurial awareness and initiatives at all industry and official platforms have been undertaken thereby creating a buzz around Youth Entrepreneurial development.

The efforts have not been limited to building awareness and training teachers but the organisation has also established several initiatives to support the young entrepreneurs and help incubate their projects. They have also introduced the concept of mentoring and training the Youth entrepreneurs by providing them with business management skills. The most effective action has been to support micro-credit projects promoted by Youth Entrepreneurs.

Recognising the importance of introducing Enterprise education amongst the youth, countries like US, Canada and Australia have already inculcated Business Management studies as a part of the normal curriculum in the education system and have also established specialised higher education courses that help create well informed, well trained and wise entrepreneurs who are able to take the lead in creating and establishing new ventures and growing them into organisations that create and provide more jobs in the market.

Globally education system is still not equipped to inculcate Enterprise education as a part of its normal syllabus. The reasons could be very many ranging from lack of interest from students and their parents, lack of adequate material and infrastructure for training, absence of qualified and suitable teaching faculty and many more reasons. However in the field of higher education we see the education in the Universities being integrated with industry where in Corporate provide required support and participate with students in their projects and studies.

Quoting Henry Ford - "A country's competitiveness starts not on the factory floor or in the engineering lab. It starts in the classroom."

Nurturing Youth Entrepreneurship - The Need of the Hour

Nurturing Youth Entrepreneurship can be highly beneficial for the society, economy as well as for the progress of the nation besides the individual's self development and achievement too. In the current times where the nations are transitioning through tough times and adapting to globalisation, the hope for the youth lies more in becoming job creators rather than job seekers. Promoting Youth Entrepreneurship helps solve a lot of problems in the society too by ensuring that the marginalised youth is brought to the main stream through providing them with self employment opportunities.

Most nations have recognised this fact and are providing some focus and thought into building programs conducive for Youth Entrepreneurship and providing the right environment for YE (Youth Entrepreneurship) to evolve. However nurturing YE calls for a strategic plan at national levels. Planning to promoting YE has got to be a multi pronged strategy of building awareness, providing role models, encouraging entrepreneurial culture, introducing Entrepreneurial developmental programmes at school and college levels as well as providing for policy framework and mentorship to encourage YE and start up businesses etc. YE building program calls for long term approach along with short term action plans too.

At a global level YEN - Youth Employment Network established up by consortium of UN, ILO & World bank works with various Governments to promote Youth Employment opportunities, promote Youth Entrepreneurship and Enterprise Building. YEN engages the various countries and their Governments by providing policy advice, help build pilot projects, imparting training and help create platforms for training the Youth.

From a Youth Entrepreneurship perspective YEN has strategically identified four areas of focus that needs to be adapted and focussed upon by all the nations. Employability, Equal opportunities for Man and Women, Entrepreneurship and Employment creation. The guideline for an implementation plan comes from addressing Employability issue and this would be the starting point of Youth Entrepreneurship building program at National level.

Strategy to develop Youth Entrepreneurship needs to first address two main areas of creating awareness and building a suitable environment as well as culture and secondly of building Entrepreneurship skill and training as a part of education at High school and University levels.

Introducing Youth Entrepreneurship awareness building program at School and college levels can ignite young

minds to understand and wake up to unlimited and undreamt of possibilities that they have in becoming self employed entrepreneurs. The awareness building program should introduce them to Entrepreneurship as an option of building their carrier, provide an understanding of business opportunities, introduce concept of business, business economics, skills and abilities required for managing and growing a business, what are the personal skills and leadership qualities they need to develop to be successful entrepreneurs etc. Once they have an idea of the opportunities that are available to them and they get a general idea of how to go about in a business environment, it is likely that the hidden potential amongst the Youth will start getting a chance to express itself and they start dreaming of becoming entrepreneurs, in which case they are likely to chart out their path for future studies that will help them equip themselves to becoming good entrepreneurs and business managers.

Three Stage Transitional Phase in Youth Entrepreneurship

Nurturing and Building Youth Entrepreneurship has got to be a long term developmental program with strategic focus and policy framework at the National Government level identifying specific areas and programs to nurture and build awareness of amongst the Youth, train and enhance their skills required for starting business enterprise. This calls for including Youth Entrepreneurship building as a regular curriculum at high school and University levels throughout the country. Secondly there has to be a common YE program involving all NGOs, Societies and Communities to create an environment and culture that is conducive to Youth Entrepreneurship. The effort of building YE does not stop with this.

There has got to be sustained campaign in media and other forms of communication to show to the Youth some of the successful role models that they can emulate. Besides Government has got to set up the required framework and policies to provide assistance required for Young Entrepreneurs to start businesses. Besides training Youth and equipping them with Business skills, there is a need to provide guidance, mentoring as well as provide assistance in start up financing and help them market themselves by providing them the opportunities at various trade forums. These are but a few of the action plans that are outlined here to help kick start Youth Entrepreneurship development strategy and programs.

In the long run the effort in this direction has to be sustained with the same enthusiasm and many more action plans involving various other agencies and fields have got to be built into the programs.

To help build Entrepreneurship awareness programs as a part of Education, it helps to understand how the Youth Entrepreneurship develops and progresses in the early years. Chigunta has proposed a **three stage transitional phase in**

Youth Entrepreneurship. Of course the stages can vary depending upon local environment and cultural factors in different countries.

1. **Pre-Entrepreneurs:** The onset of this stage starts at 15 years up to 19 years. This is the stage when the youth is leaving home and starts identifying himself as an individual. His thoughts and ideas about his future and career start forming at this stage. Entrepreneurial attitudes are formed naturally or as a result of awareness programs and honed from this stage onwards.

2. **Budding entrepreneurs:** This stage lasts from 20-25 years. During this period the youth would have tried their hand at some kind of work or tried to start and run a small business. Whether they manage to succeed or burn their fingers, they will have acquired the practical knowhow and pitfalls of Entrepreneurship and the outside world.

3. **Emergent entrepreneurs:** Youth between the ages of 26 to 29 years fall into this category. By this time they would have had the necessary experience, made mistakes and realised what it takes to manage a business. They are more likely to be grounded, realistic and ready to prepare and start their enterprise on more mature and sure footage with good lot of preparation and wisdom.

The above classification can help us understand the growing up trends amongst the youth and help us design policies and programs more effectively. Providing the right input at the right time helps the Youth assimilate the necessary information in a better way and use it effectively.

Access To Finance - Barrier to Youth Entrepreneurship Development

When the countries are focussed on creating and nurturing an environment conducive to Youth Entrepreneurship, it becomes imperative to study the current situation, identify the pitfalls and shortcomings and design new strategies to overcome and remove the obstacles and make the path easier and clear for the youth to pursue. The other area of importance happens to be **to educate and empower the youth with the required knowledge, skills and training to enable them to become successful entrepreneurs**.

When an interest in pursuing a new enterprise or becoming self employed has been generated in a young individual, he or she is likely to attend various courses and equip themselves with the required skill sets and knowledge to start the business. Identifying a good and viable business opportunity and proposition too can happen with a bit of market research and mentoring by the experienced entrepreneurs. When it comes to start the action towards setting up the business enterprise, the next set of barriers or obstacles will need to be surmounted. These barriers are mainly to do with financing options and documentation requirements. As the youth are inexperienced, they are unable to cope up with the requirements and find it difficult to get going smoothly.

Financial Barriers

Personal Savings & Borrowings from Family and Friends

In most cases the youth do not have any avenues for saving money and accumulating the margin money needed for business. They are often required to raise the initial capital through the support of family and friends. In such cases the amount of funds that can be put together would be meagre and not sufficient to get going. Very often the youth would have to repay the education loan taken for funding their studies and hence will already be in debt servicing mode leaving no possibilities for saving any money. Such youth are not considered to be safe and are perceived to be potential risk by the bankers.

Even if the youth has a very good business opportunity, the required technical knowledge and other capabilities to make it a success, financing the business becomes a major hurdle.

Borrowing From FI & Banks

The next option for the youth to finance their business venture is to approach banks and financial institutions to raise the required capital in the form of loan.

- Borrowing from Commercial Financial institution calls for providing personal securities and guarantees. Normally youth will not be in a position to provide such securities and will not have the personal credibility to be eligible for securing loans easily.

- In most cases youth lack the knowledge of debt financing, working capital management and the overall impact of financial management. It is quite possible that their financial estimates could be way off the mark. They can get carried away and plan a higher estimate or under estimate the capital requirement due to in experience.

- Banks and financial institutions as well as the other funding agencies are found to be very strict and conservative in processing the applications, ascertaining eligibility of the borrower and tend to be very stringent in their approach to funding the Youth in their first venture.

- Time taken to obtain financial support and to complete the required documentation can cause a lot of delay. If the time taken to process runs into a couple of months, the business plans of the Young Entrepreneur will definitely get affected.

- Lack of knowledge of legal procedures to start an enterprise and the required licenses, permits etc cause in-ordinate delays in documentation when it comes to loan processing by the banks.

Overall, the youth find it very difficult to access finances for their start up ventures. Sometimes such difficulties can kill the entrepreneurial spirit or one could end up losing the business opportunity due to inordinate delays in arranging funding to kick start the business. This is the area where the Governments can get involved and help make it easier by providing solutions through special seed funding agencies, micro financing organisations and similar such networks that can back up the first time ventures of Young Entrepreneurs.

Improving Access to Finance for Young Entrepreneurs

Youth Entrepreneurship development calls for support from various quarters. Primarily the need exists to initiate a Youth Entrepreneurship culture and drive amongst the youth in the society. The youth needs to think and aspire to be entrepreneurs and explore their potentials to the maximum. At the second stage, Youth Entrepreneurship nurturing calls for promoting awareness and providing training through education. The youth who wish to pursue their own business would need to hone their skills and enhance their knowledge on how to start and grow a business enterprise.

Nurturing Youth Entrepreneurship does not end with providing training to the youth. **There needs to be a sustained effort through providing regulatory framework and dedicated support systems and tools to help finance the start up ventures by providing the seed capital at economical costs.** Many countries have set up specialised funding agencies that focus on providing financial assistance in the form of loans, subsidies, debt re-financing options etc. to the first time Young entrepreneurs. In the current times we see venture capitalists looking out for bright and young entrepreneurs with fantastic business ideas to finance and help them get started. Such funding of brand new business ventures is becoming common in the high tech, IT and Service Sectors.

Grants & Subsidies

Normally in various countries, the Youth Entrepreneurship funding happens through three types of financial aid mechanisms. The normal options available are Free Grants, Fee Money & Debt financing |equity financing. In developed countries there exist various systems of providing grants to the new entrepreneurs to help them tide over their livelihood and initial expenses of starting a business venture. Many academicians argue that providing free money or grant does not help the business venture and might go into expenses that are not related directly to the business venture at hand.

The Princes Trust, Sistea de Apojo aos Jovens Empraserios [SAJE] in Itality, UK & Portugal and The Imprenditorialita Giovanile [IG] in Italy are some of the corporations and institutions that provide grants to encourage Youth Entrepreneurship. IG-Italy, provides grants and free financial subsidies to youth entrepreneurs in the age group of 18 to 35 to start their own ventures. They provide subsidies to cover up to sixty percent of the seed capital requirement of the business proposal. Prince's Trust Business Program in UK supports Young Entrepreneurs with test marketing grants up to £ 1500.00. SAJE in Portugal provides grants to cover fifty percent of the capital and additional ten percent subsidies depending upon the specific region where the business is going to be located. The subsidies can amount upto €50,000 depending upon each business case.

In all cases where grants are provided to Youth Entrepreneurs, the conditions and criteria as well as the norms and documentation are likely to be very high and the selection process equally strict and lengthy. Obtaining free grants and subsidies is not easy and is very time consuming. In general it might be easier for entrepreneurs to search for commercial borrowing and other funding options than to depend solely on the free grants.

Finance Counselling & Assistance

There exist several agencies and non profit organisations that help young entrepreneurs by providing them, guiding and helping them with preparing their business proposals, researching on finance options available and help prepare the project reports and recommendations to help with the sourcing of funds.

Soft Loans & Micro Finance

In most of the developed and developing countries, banks and financial institutions are offering soft loans to the Young entrepreneurs in a bid to develop the new sector. Soft loans to Young Entrepreneurs are provided at reduced rate of interest or the debt is structure in a way as to postpone the interest payments. The banks also go easy on the collateral and other documentation requirements in a bid to be more Customer friendly.

Micro Financing has caught up in a big way in most countries. Micro financing organisations are normally social enterprises like NGOs or Credit Unions and Trusts with a vast exposure and network in rural areas covering both organised and informal sectors. Young entrepreneurs find it a lot easier to obtain small loans without many hassles of collateral and documentation. If the capital required is relatively small, then Micro financing option suites very well.

Venture Capital & Angel Investors

Private Fund Managers and Angel Investors looking for opportunities to invest have woken up to the unlimited possibilities of funding some of the brightest and the best business ideas in the upcoming hi tech sectors like IT, medical sciences, bio-technology as well as other sectors like service sector, commercial R&D etc. The companies who backed first time entrepreneurs and business ventures like Hotmail, Google, Face book and many more technology companies have reaped rich rewards. Having smelt the success, they are focussing on picking up bright and innovative entrepreneurs and helping them incubate their business ventures. Any Young Entrepreneur with the required technical knowledge, bright and innovative business idea need not look to banks for finance but he will find the VCs knocking at his door to partner with him.

Administrative & Regulatory Environment and Youth Entrepreneurship

Most countries have recognised the need to provide focus and assistance to building Youth Entrepreneurship in their societies. A lot of effort has gone into building and nurturing Entrepreneurial spirit through education at school and college levels. Such efforts have also been backed up with specific training programs and media campaigns to sustain the effort in encouraging and empowering Youth entrepreneurship.

A lot of researchers have focussed on understanding the barriers and obstacles faced by Young Entrepreneurs in their efforts to start their own enterprise. Apart from lack of the required business skills and knowledge, non availability of easy debt financing schemes and administrative formalities have emerged as the major obstacles deterring the Youth from attempting to start their businesses in formal sectors. Many prefer to start small ventures in informal sector thus avoiding getting into the documentation and procedures required for bigger enterprises.

Administrative & Registration Requirements

In case of developed countries, the regulatory environment and the business compliance requirements are very many and complex. A lot of time and effort needs to be spent continually by the entrepreneur in order to be compliant. The cost and effort of becoming compliant involves a lot of time which the entrepreneur can ill afford. To start a new business venture one needs to go through numerous administrative processes to obtain business registration, licenses, deal with legal and copyrights, building approvals and permits, obtaining clearances from municipalities as well as safety and HR compliance in all respects. The list of agencies and departments involved and the compliance process can be varied and numerous. The number of registration requirement from various agencies varies from country to country, from minimum of two up to twenty registrations in countries like Uganda, Paraguay etc. While there are no administrative costs involved in such registrations in some countries like Denmark, the same costs can be very high in few other countries like Yemen, Syria etc. In case of new entrepreneurs, they lack the knowledge as well as the time and resources to follow through all the procedures while having to attend to other more pressing matters of their business. Very often small time entrepreneurs are likely to overlook or get into informal sector and get into grey market where they find it easier to operate and earn profits in a short term. If an individual were to take up this route, there is little chance that he will establish and grow an organisation in future.

Bankruptcy Laws

Bankruptcy laws in several countries are very severe when it comes to the penalties imposed on businesses that go bankrupt and fail. The cost aspect along with the inordinate delays and time taken in the procedures can prove to be an inhibitor to youth entrepreneurs who would rather play safe than take such personal risks. Business failures are very real and the youth at an age group of 18 to 29 years do not have sufficient experience and confidence to back them up. Not all youth are reckless and risk taking when it comes to choosing a self employment opportunity with such risks.

Copyright, Patent & Trademark Regulations

Many young entrepreneurs who have started their own ventures to promote their innovative products, designs and software etc have found it very hard and expensive to deal with Copyright and Patent issues. Obtaining patents is a very expensive proposition and time consuming too. In technology and other areas like pharma and medical sciences, young entrepreneurs can loose out on their inventions and products to competition and bigger players due to their inability to obtain patents in time.

Youth Entrepreneurship and Business Support

We are living in exciting times. Technology, globalisation and advancement in all fields has ushered a new age where lifestyle is going to be redefined. Internet has changed the face of the earth. It has managed to erase the borders and nationalities to bring all of humanity on one platform. Internet also provides unlimited opportunities to the youth for starting ones own business enterprise rather than seek jobs. Whether one is good in technology, trading, product development or any field, there are unlimited opportunities to build a successful venture if one has the entrepreneurial drive.

While recognising the need and the potential of Youth Entrepreneurship world over, ILO and other Agencies have begun to focus on establishing programs to help create, nurture and support Youth Entrepreneurship world over. The effort to encourage the YE culture has got to be done by the countries themselves.

In trying to address the YE program, several studies have been conducted to identify the areas where YE needs to be supported, identify the barriers to YE in the societies and to develop implementation strategies to help build Youth Entrepreneurship.

For a Youth Entrepreneur, starting an own business can be quite an overwhelming exercise. Though he or she might have a good business idea or identified opportunity, the lack of experience and exposure to business world can level them running around the pillar trying to set up a business organisation and get going. The challenges of starting a business are many. When an individual is starting an enterprise, he has got to handle all matters of organisation including administration, accounting, taxation, production, purchase, marketing and all jobs by himself. Having no previous experience, he has got to learn the ropes of the business and find out how things work. At this stage one needs help in the form of business support, mentoring and supporting network that can help him get going and learn the ropes faster too.

Apart from the other areas like finance, marketing, regulatory requirements and registration etc, where the Young Entrepreneurs are needed to be trained and assisted, they will also need support and assistance on how to get the business started and get going.

Lack of Business Contacts - In the start up stage, the YE is not aware of the suppliers and customers in the market. Identifying and understanding the procurement market and getting to know the customer markets can take quite a while. It is a lot easier if at this stage business specific support and information were to be extended through advisory bodies. Readily available information and industry contacts can make it a lot easier and faster for the YE to move ahead in setting up the operations and get going.

Business/Industry Specific Business Assistance

Every business has its own way of business operations and culture. Providing exposure to industry specific processes, introduction to the markets and suppliers including the common methodology and procedures of doing business can make it a lot easier for the YE saving a lot of his time. Such support can be made available through Government support agencies and specific Trade bodies with trained workers and researchers with experience.

Mentoring

If Young Entrepreneurs were to be provided access to mentors and experienced business entrepreneurs, it would help YE receive not only the practical guidance and wisdom to get going and avoid mistakes but their confidence as well as the speed at which they can move ahead in their business will be enhanced. The mentors have been there and done that and hence are in a position to guide the YE in the right way wherein costly mistakes and delays can be avoided and the YE gets to climb the learning curve faster.

In the mentors happen to be from the same line of business as the YE, then the value of such an association can be much higher for the Mentor can introduce the YE to the market and the industry and support in giving the leads.

Infrastructure Support

YE in the initial stages would require a lot of help in setting up an office and get started. Most often they lack the resources to fund for the basic infrastructure. Providing working space and common administrative support in the early stages can help the YE immensely for they not only save on spending the money on infrastructure and can invest into the business but they save time and effort in setting up the infrastructure support too.

SAYES Australia [South Australian Youth Entrepreneur Scheme] is a project sponsored by South Australian Business community which is designed to support the youth in the age of 18 to 30 years in their endeavour to become entrepreneurs.

The entire business community is engaged in encouraging the youth build on their business ideas, provide the requisite training and support and mentor them. The youth has access to the entire business community and the network through SAYES. With selected Young Entrepreneurs, SAYES engages in mentoring, assisting in building the business plan and proposal as well as providing financial, legal and statutory compliance advice. They introduce the YE to the network of businessmen members in the industry and such contacts are of immense help to the beginners. SAYES also conducts business skills and other related trainings and conferences for Young Entrepreneurs. In some cases the agency also provides financial assistance depending upon the eligibility criteria and the business case.

In conclusion we can say that there is a lot that the business community and experienced veterans can contribute and lead the Young Entrepreneurs until they learn the ropes of the business. It is for the Youth to realise this and see value in receiving guidance.

Starting an enterprise with meagre resources and no background experience is very tough indeed. Government and other business networks have a lot to contribute and assist YE in getting started by means of providing common shared resources and infrastructure at affordable prices or free of cost.

Youth Entrepreneurship Building Skills

Building a society that is responsive to, encouraging and favourable to Youth Entrepreneurship is the responsibility of every society as well as the Government. **Encouraging the Youth to become entrepreneurs has a lot of advantages in terms of solving problems of unemployment in the economy as well as paving way for the innovation and growth of the country too**. Understanding the need to creating and nurturing Youth Entrepreneurship, many countries have taken up strategic initiatives and implemented plans aimed at imparting Entrepreneurial skills and knowledge through education. Such a move no doubt provides the freedom and the thrust to the Youth to dream and achieve their dreams.

Leadership is not only a born talent but can be acquired through learning and training too. An ideal entrepreneurial training and studies should include subjects like Entrepreneurship Awareness Building Skills, Entrepreneurial & Personal Empowerment skills, Business Planning, Business Management as well as Personal Empowerment skills.

Entrepreneurship Awareness Building

Entrepreneurship is all about being a visionary self starter leadership, one who is able to identify opportunities to offer solutions in the form of product, technology, process or service to fulfil a need and thereby gather and employ all necessary resources including manpower, finance, technology, infrastructure and others to build a successful enterprise in the chosen area of business.

Being an entrepreneur calls for a lot of grit and determination as well as ability to take calculated risks as well as responsibility. Leadership calls for the ability to find workable solutions and crossing all hurdles to reach the goal without getting bogged down. An entrepreneur carries a vision not only of making profits but has a larger vision of creating jobs, helping people develop their potential, contributing to the society and at the same time ensuring the growth of his or her organisation and the people connected.

At the initial stage, one might have an inclination towards becoming an entrepreneur. But normally the students will not have an idea of what it means to be an entrepreneur. Such an awareness program educating them and introducing the concept of entrepreneurship in schools and colleges as well as through dedicated training programs help the youth make up their minds to pursue entrepreneurship as an option to a career.

Entrepreneurial Building

Being an entrepreneur calls for playing a multi disciplinary and multi functional role in managing one's enterprise. A successful entrepreneur is able to not only identify business opportunities, but is enterprising in his approach to developing the business opportunities into successful business enterprise. This calls for thinking out of the box and extraordinary leadership, creativity, foresight, ability to think ahead, ability to create options, ability to gather resources, manage resources to achieve the target as well as negotiate and solve problems both internal to the business as well as with external environment. Being enterprising is an attitude of the mind. A good entrepreneur looks not only at his success, but the success of his organisation as well as of the team that works with him. Entrepreneurship is also about being able to attract the best talent, to provide leadership and guidance to grow and nurture the talent, manage and harness the talent pool too. Through training one who has a basic initiative towards entrepreneurship can be moulded to become a successful entrepreneur. Ability to think creatively, looking at the macro and micro environment as well as options, negotiating with alternatives and managing processes on all fronts without losing out on the vision can be sharpened through Entrepreneurial training.

Personal Empowerment Skills

Personal empowerment and development is necessary for every individual and most importantly for an entrepreneur. These skills apply to one's ability to perform in his |her work area. One needs to have the specific job function or technical skill to pursue a particular vocation but along with the functional skill and knowledge it is the personal empowerment of the individual that helps him succeed in the enterprise.

Personal Empower skills training imparts mind training to the entrepreneur, helping him learn to focus, concentrate, analyse and be objective in his thinking. Positive thinking, learning to be assertive and affirmative as well as being balanced in thinking at all times, being calmly active, ability to manage stress and work under pressure are some of the skills that are a must for every successful entrepreneur.

An entrepreneur is also a leader. Through training he can develop leadership skills as well as groom oneself and build a positive image as well as enhance one's self esteem. Personal development in the areas of self discipline, time management, being self-motivated and enthusiast are very essential for a young entrepreneur who is making his foray into business. All these skills can be learnt through specific training.

A good leader is assertive and at the same time able to motivate and encourage the others too. He has got to have excellent listening skills, patience & wisdom, emotional intelligence and more importantly a Win-Win attitude towards life and work.

A entrepreneur who is able to think big for oneself and for all of his team and take the entire organisation to reach the heights and realise their potential is a successful individual too. To become a good visionary entrepreneur, training helps for it helps sharpen his abilities, build additional skills as well as make him bring out his true potential too.

Approach to Youth Entrepreneurship Policy Making

Youth is one of the prime and most important human resources of each and every nation. Providing growth opportunities, enabling and equipping the youth with skills required for acquiring professional qualifications as well as building entrepreneurial capabilities is one of the prime areas of focus of every country to harness the potential available. Building youth entrepreneurship has several benefits for the society and the youth too. Any initiative and implementation of action plan in this direction calls for policy directives from the government.

Governments of all countries have started focusing on Youth entrepreneurship in the recent years thanks to the research and study by the academician, NGOs and International Organizations. In all countries the Governments have realized the need for policy making in the field of Youth entrepreneurship with an aim to solve some of the unemployment problems amongst the youth, bring marginalized youth into the main stream and provide them with gainful avenues of employment as well as for the overall benefit and advancement of the society too. The policy making in this area is still in its nascent stages and is evolving.

Drawing up Youth Entrepreneurship policy calls for collaboration and integration from multiple stake holders in the society, Government as well as other sectors including NGOs, Education, Labour and Youth

Departments. The youth policy would have to be drawn up taking into account the social, financial, political as well as micro and macroeconomic policies with both short term as well as long term perspectives. Political will and initiative at all levels of the Government, Industry as well as society can go a long way in providing the right impetus for the growth of Youth Entrepreneurship in the country.

Needless to mention that the Youth Entrepreneurship policy making has to originate at the national level and by consensus. The policy directives and initiatives should then be driven down to the regional and local levels. Drawing up national policy on Youth Entrepreneurship would need to take into consideration the international organization's outlook and policies concerning the Youth and align with the same as far as possible. Keeping in line with ILO's policy guidelines concerning Youth Entrepreneurship and employment, in country policies can aim to create increased employment opportunities as well as increase the capability of the youth and provide direction for the growth of Youth Power.

Youth Entrepreneurial policy would be unique for each and every country as its socio- economic framework and society are different in each case would determine the kind of policy the country would need to adopt. Every society and youth would have its unique features and characteristics besides the economic factors that would have to be taken into account to draw up policy measures as applicable to the current times as well as with long term perspective.

Policy making in Youth Entrepreneurship calls for understanding the current dynamics, the emerging scenarios in the society and other related fields including economy, industry, education etc, understanding problems amongst the youth in all sections of society as well as futuristic trends and developing suitable interventions to address the problems as well as to embark on a comprehensive and futuristic policy.

Youth Entrepreneurship Policy Making - A Perspective

Keeping in line with the ILO and UN Organizations focus and emphasis in the area of Youth Entrepreneurship, several countries have begun to work towards designing policy framework for developing Youth Entrepreneurship in the country.

Academicians and several agencies have invested into studying and bringing out a lot of data and information defining Youth entrepreneurship and have suggested policy approach too. Youth entrepreneurship policies are defined at the national level by the Government in collaboration with several departments including Youth affairs, Education, Finance and other related disciplines to ensure that the complete needs of Youth are addressed to while defining the policy.

Accordingly, **Youth Entrepreneurship of countries take into account and define policies that address the entire process of building the skills and providing the education**

to equip youth with necessary technical, business, finance, training and other related areas to prepare them to embark on entrepreneurship.

A comprehensive youth entrepreneurship policy goes on to the next phase of developing and grooming the Youth in terms of soft skills including, attitude, motivation and ethics etc. The policy should include specific actions that will increase the employability of the youth in measurable terms.

A progressive Youth Entrepreneurial policy goes on further to describe and define several kinds of entrepreneurial opportunities and sectors that are available to the Youth and provide for training and guidance to the youth to equip themselves for each of the identified sectors.

An effective Youth Entrepreneurship policy should include the provisions and schemes that the Government intends to make available to the youth by means of providing assistance in the areas of finance, guidance, mentoring, single window clearance, marketing and sales assistance as well as technical assistance in all areas of business operations to encourage and incubate youth entrepreneurs.

It should be understood very clearly that in every country, it is the Government that needs to create the avenues and opportunities for employment as well as for entrepreneurship and educate, train as well as equip the youth to take on the opportunities. How and when this can be achieved would become the important part of the policy that will define the road ahead that leads to implementation.

As the Youth Entrepreneurship policy involves multiple sectors, it is important to make the budgetary provisions as well as define the responsibilities of each and every other department and outline a collaborative approach to the overall implementation of policy guidelines.

Youth entrepreneurships form a part of the overall economy and the industrial segments. SMEs and service sectors that are predominantly private enterprises do contribute to the overall economy both in financial perspective as well as from the point of service perspective as well. Therefore a huge part of the economic policy towards SME development goes hand in hand with Youth entrepreneurship policy as well.

Thus Youth Entrepreneurship policy definition needs to be all comprehensive and futuristic encompassing education, economy, social and other related fields outlining action plan and time frame for achieving the goals. In current times where countries are undergoing economic as well as social and cultural changes due to the evolution of technology and globalization, the YE policies would need to take into account the changes happening in the society and amongst the youth and be able to address their aspirations and provide them with a map to the future that will unleash the Youth power.

Youth power if harnessed guided and nurtured carefully, will certainly contribute to the growth of the society and the nation undoubtedly. Therefore Youth Entrepreneurship policy demands such focus and importance in every country.

Stake Holders in Youth Entrepreneurship Development Policy

Youth Entrepreneurship development in any country calls for Macro and Micro level detailing and policy definition. **Effectiveness in implementation of Youth Entrepreneurship depends chiefly on the policy definition, provisions and the implementation plan envisaged as per the policy. One of the most important aspects of Youth Entrepreneurship development that one needs to keep in mind while drafting the policy is to ensure that all key stakeholders roles and responsibilities are defined.** Though the policy is defined by the Government of each country, the implementation is facilitated through and by the stake holders. Therefore the stake holders play a very critical role in the entire program and if not addressed adequately can lead to becoming barriers in the implementation.

Government - The Primary Stake Holder

First and foremost the primary and most important stake holders in Youth Entrepreneurship development policy program happens to be the Government. When we refer to the Government, it should be noted that the Federal or Central Government defines and brings out the policy. However the policy directives are then carried forward and taken up by the regional and local Governments as well as the local Youth Departments of the Government.

In building a culture that promotes Youth Entrepreneurship development in the country, the Government at all levels has a major role to play by creating the right environment, providing the impetus to the movement and initiating a positive and developmental language and culture. The different departments and ministries under the Government concerned with Youth, Education and other related areas also form an extension of the Government's arm.

Private Sector Enterprises

Apart from the Government and the related institutions which own the Youth Entrepreneurship development responsibility, the private sector and the society too has an equally important role in this area. By Private sector we are referring to the entire industry including the banking and financial institutions, the trade associations, the general trade, the industries and all private institutions including educational institutions and establishments. Effective implementation in Youth Entrepreneurship development calls for providing & creating opportunities for the Youth to get engaged in entrepreneurship can be done only by these private stake holders.

In a culture that is pro Youth Entrepreneurship, we find the industry and the private companies coming forward to encourage the Youth, to hand hold and give them opportunities to get started as entrepreneurs. The business leaders too take a personal interest in this area and motivate the Youth in the right direction. Some of the corporate business houses take it as their social responsibility to provide and encourage the Youth Entrepreneurship. Some of the Multi National Companies like IBM etc are known to support women and youth entrepreneurs actively in developing countries and reserve few areas of services procurement to the Youth thereby encouraging them to become service providers to the Company.

Non Profit Sector - The Facilitators

Apart from the Government and the Private sector players, it is the Non-profit sector organizations such as the NGOs, The Youth Organizations, Community Networks, Cultural Associations and Private Trusts and Foundations that play the important role of being facilitators and enablers of Youth Entrepreneurship Policy implementation. These stake holders can be said to be the movers and shakers of the YE Programs in the society. The NGOs contribute a lot not only by way of engaging directly in the implementation and working with Youth groups but also by way of engaging in field studies, providing valuable data and assessment to the study groups.

Finally the Youth Power belongs to the society and by promoting Youth Entrepreneurship, the entire society including the public and media, as well as the nation is benefitted. Therefore we can rightly say that the society too is a stake holder in the policy implementation in the country.

The Difference Between Running Your Own Business and Working for One

Entrepreneurship is by definition risky and an entrepreneur is one who takes risk with either his or her money or money raised from financial institutions and venture capitalists. Hence, entrepreneurs must keep in mind the fact that they need to be cautious and prudent about their ventures as failure means that they must take the responsibility and unlike employees, who can find other jobs, the entrepreneurs have to live with bad credit history which in turn leads to lack of financing from institutions. Of course, all this is when the entrepreneur starts his or her business and before that, the task of raising capital is by itself such a huge task that many potential entrepreneurs fail at this step itself. The key to raising capital from venture capitalists and angel investors is by having a compelling and innovative idea and by having a well thought out business plan. More often than not, potential entrepreneurs think that they have a great idea without doing their homework, which a seasoned venture capitalist would immediately shoot down. Further, many entrepreneurs do not develop well thought out business plans that do not take into account all aspects of running the business including revenue projections, break even timelines, the market potential, and more importantly the cash flows that are so integral to keeping the business afloat.

Some Tips for Aspiring Entrepreneurs

To take each of these aspects in turn, we find that having a realistic projection of future revenues is very important as it gives a basis to the proposal from the entrepreneur. In other words, unless there is a clearly defined roadmap to the breakeven point and the projection of revenues that is practical and based on solid market statistics and consumer behavior, the business plan would not be feasible. After all which financial institution or bank or venture capitalist would put their money into a venture that does not have a plan for returns and profits that is not based on airy fairy dreams but on data. Apart from this, the entrepreneur has to manage the working capital requirements in an astute and financially savvy manner. Research has shown that most ventures fail because a year or two into the business, they face liquidity crunches and are unable to meet the working capital requirements needed to keep their venture afloat. Managing and projecting cash flows are two different things and while one can project huge cash flows, managing the actual receivables and honoring the payables are entirely different aspects. One should not be forced to windup one's business because the payables are more than the receivables by too high a margin. Alternatively, the payables are coming due and the receivables are getting piled up without any hope for collection.

Some Dilemmas Faced by Entrepreneurs

The other aspect about entrepreneurship is the staffing factor. The dilemma of choosing staff and employees whose loyalty to the entrepreneur and commitment to the venture versus hiring staff who are high fliers but who might overrule the entrepreneurs is a key aspect. Of course, this does not mean that the venture must be staffed only by yes men or those who cannot find employment anywhere else. Rather, the point here is that the question of whom the entrepreneur trusts is paramount and hence, the staffing must be done after doing due diligence. Further, bringing in outside talent as opposed to appointing family members and friends to key positions is another aspect that needs careful deliberation and conscious application of one's mind to the hiring of staff.

Closing Thoughts

Finally, entrepreneurs must be on the lookout for corporate predators who once they realize that the venture is doing great, might invest substantial money into taking over the venture. This has happened in practice across the world and the strategy of the entrepreneurs in this case was to hold the majority stake in the venture and keep management control and retain shareholding patterns tightly and closely.

www.ingramcontent.com/pod-product-compliance
Lightning Source LLC
Chambersburg PA
CBHW080824180526
45168CB00006B/2561